YOUR KNOWLEDGE HAS VALUE

- We will publish your bachelor's and
  master's thesis, essays and papers

- Your own eBook and book -
  sold worldwide in all relevant shops

- Earn money with each sale

Upload your text at www.GRIN.com
and publish for free

Bibliographic information published by the German National Library:

The German National Library lists this publication in the National Bibliography; detailed bibliographic data are available on the Internet at http://dnb.dnb.de .

This book is copyright material and must not be copied, reproduced, transferred, distributed, leased, licensed or publicly performed or used in any way except as specifically permitted in writing by the publishers, as allowed under the terms and conditions under which it was purchased or as strictly permitted by applicable copyright law. Any unauthorized distribution or use of this text may be a direct infringement of the author s and publisher s rights and those responsible may be liable in law accordingly.

Imprint:

Copyright © 2016 GRIN Verlag, Open Publishing GmbH
Print and binding: Books on Demand GmbH, Norderstedt Germany
ISBN: 9783668326880

This book at GRIN:

http://www.grin.com/en/e-book/341961/special-educational-needs-intervention-to-promote-pupils-in-their-learning

Laura Imperatori

Special Educational Needs. Intervention to promote pupils in their learning

GRIN Publishing

GRIN - Your knowledge has value

Since its foundation in 1998, GRIN has specialized in publishing academic texts by students, college teachers and other academics as e-book and printed book. The website www.grin.com is an ideal platform for presenting term papers, final papers, scientific essays, dissertations and specialist books.

Visit us on the internet:

http://www.grin.com/

http://www.facebook.com/grincom

http://www.twitter.com/grin_com

University of Manchester

PGCE

Secondary Written Assignment 3

Special Educational Needs

How can I intervene to promote my pupils in their learning according to their Special Educational Needs?

Author:
Laura IMPERATORI

Institution:
TEACH FIRST NORTH WEST

What theories influenced your practice in order to improve the learning of a pupil you need to teach with a specific learning need or more pupils you teach with a similar specific educational need?

29th September 2016

SPECIAL EDUCATIONAL NEEDS ASSIGNMENT

ABSTRACT. Every individual has different learning strengths and weaknesses; however, some have more exceptional abilities for or more barriers to learning. Learners can also be 'twice exceptional', such as the individual chosen for this intervention. He is a gifted Y7 Science pupil with dyslexic tendencies. Based on my baseline assessment, he fits most closely into the dysphonetic dyslexia subgroup. The depicted intervention was based on identifying his strengths and weaknesses and aimed to develop his literacy skills, especially his phonological awareness, as well as his interest and understanding of science simultaneously. The effectiveness of the intervention was assessed using a Before-and-After comparison of a written summary. In the final assessment, the pupil made fewer spelling mistakes and was more able to correct them independently. More precisely, the literacy error ratio, as calculated by dividing the number of erroneous words by the total number of words, improved from 15.78% to 9.46%. Moreover, the overall structure of his summary was better organised, using the DEFENDS method he was taught.

Date: 29th September 2016.

Contents

> *"Intellectually gifted individuals with specific learning disabilities are the most misjudged, misunderstood, and neglected segment of the student population and the community. Teachers, school counsellors, and others often overlook the signs of intellectual giftedness and focus attention on such deficits as poor spelling, reading, and writing."*

Whitmore & Maker, 1985

Special Educational Needs are a very wide range of different additional needs of learners that teachers need to address in an inclusive school. In this study, we are focussing on one gifted and able pupil that most likely suffers from dysphonetic dyslexia, a specific subtype of dyslexia. Currently, he has not got an educational statement for secondary school; however, he was classified as SEN in Primary School. Furthermore, his understanding of Science is significantly greater than his spelling abilities are.

1. INTRODUCTION

1.1. **Dyslexia.** According to the World Health Organisation (2010), "Dyslexia is a brain-based condition. It is a disorder manifested by difficulty in learning to read, despite conventional instructions, adequate intelligence and socio-cultural opportunity. It is dependent upon fundamental cognitive disabilities which are of constitutional origin." This implies that – differently to the common perception of learning disorders – the occurrence of dyslexia is not correlated to IQ. Hence, there are learners that are dyslexic and highly able at the same time. Moreover, dyslexia covers a very wide range of needs. Some dyslexics have more difficulties with phonological processing, others with pattern recognition. Phonological awareness is the conscious sensitivity to the sound structure of language. It includes the ability to auditorily distinguish units of speak, such as the word's syllables and a syllable's phonemes. Pattern recognition refers to perceiving the coherent 'gestalt' of a word. Capel (2005) states that the emphasis of any intervention should be on examining the individual's skills, such as phonological awareness, and working on them as a way forward.

1.1.1. *Dyslexia subtypes.* There are several different subgroups in dyslexia. The dyslexia subtypes can be identified by investigating the different patterns of reading and spelling deficits on various diagnostic test. In 1963, Kinsbourne and Warrington identified two groups, one that suffered from a language disorder and another one from a nonverbal sequential processing difficulty. Boder and Jarrico (1962) developed a screening tool that sorts individuals into three different subgroups of dyslexia based on their strengths and weaknesses in two different forms of information processing that rely on different neurological functions. The human brain processes information very differently in different tasks. Information processing can either be based on analytic-sequential synthesis (e.g. recalling a phone number, predominant in left cerebral hemisphere) or simultaneous gestalt recognition (e.g. face recognition, mainly controlled by the right hemisphere). The dysphonetic subtype performs well in simultaneous 'gestalt' recognition, but exhibits difficulty using phonetic analysis, which corresponds to the skill of auditory analytic-sequential synthesis. This can be measured by how well phonics are applied in 'sounding-out' unknown words and in phonetically spelling unknown words. Similarly, the dyseidetic subtype has a deficit in recognising whole word configurations, or 'gestalts', but has no difficulty with phonic skills. The dyseidetic's misspellings are often phonically accurate, e.g. 'talc' for talk. Mixed dysphonetic-dyseidetic dyslexics have deficits in both key skills of information processing, resulting in great difficulties when developing sight vocabulary and phonic skills.

1.1.2. *Dyslexia in the classroom.* According to Hooper (2000), literacy skills like learning to read, spell, express one's thoughts on paper and acquire adequate use of grammar are essential tools for learning a large part of the curriculum taught at school. For dyslexic children, the acquisition of these literacy skills is not only difficult, but they can also suffer a lot of anguish and trauma when they may feel mentally abused by their peers within the school environment because of their learning difficulty. Teachers can work towards alleviating this by integrating the child into the class environment, making the respective pupils feel self-confident.

1.2. **Giftedness/Ability.** Based on Renzulli (2004), giftedness can be defined along a continuum ranging from a very conservative or restricted definition of giftedness (focussing almost exclusively on IQ test scores) to a more multi-dimensional view. The conservative view has influenced the identification of gifted pupils during the early part of the past century, is strongly correlated to 'schoolhouse giftedness' due to its emphasis on analytical and verbal skills. 'Schoolhouse giftedness' is used to mean the ability to perform well in test-taking or lesson-learning. However, divergent thinking, non-entrenchment, and creative productive giftedness are types of giftedness that are most valued by society, as they have led to major contributions to the arts and sciences (Renzulli, 1978, 1986). Moreover, Benbow and Minor (1990) showed that "... global indicators of intellectual functioning may exclude too many non-verbally gifted students, who appear to be less balanced than verbally gifted students in their cognitive development". In conclusion, although schoolhouse giftedness should be valued and accommodated, at least equal attention should be devoted to creative productive giftedness, promoting students' development of original ideas, according to Renzulli (2004). For this approach to be fruitful, student interests need to be taken into account and an investigative methodology needs to be promoted in lessons.

1.3. **Gifted and learning disabled.** Linda Kreger Silverman once stated that "it is a well-kept secret that a child can be both gifted and disabled". According to Davis (2010), dyslexics are primarily picture thinkers. Rather than using internal dialogue, they specialise in mental or sensory imagery, hence they learn to excel in spatial rather than verbal thinking. Toll (1993) differentiated three different types of gifted and learning disabled pupils: the subtle gifted LD, hidden gifted LD and the recognised learning-disabled. Based on my experience with the pupil that is taking part in this intervention, he is on the borderline between the subtle and the hidden learning disabled subgroups. However, he fits more closely into the group of the subtle gifted LD in Science, as he matches very closely with Toll's criteria, i.e. he has good verbal skills, poor spelling and handwriting, is disorganised in his classwork and the giftedness compensates for his learning disability, which might be one the reasons why his disability is not recognised. He is also viewed as 'underachieving' in English, as stated by his English teacher. His English teacher attributed his consistent underachievement to carelessness or lack of effort. According to Hooper (2000), many teachers of dyslexic children misinterpret their observations in a similar way. One of the other descriptors that I cannot verify in his specific case is whether the discrepancies between strengths and weakness widen as he grows older. In the following, it will be outlined how specific strategies can be based on this diagnosis, that promote the learner's strengths, but also work on the weaknesses. They have been first proposed in Bisland (2005).

1.4. **Diagnosis challenges.** Sah and Borland (1989) estimated that the gifted and learning-disabled subgroup is the largest of all subgroups of gifted and disabled students; however, they also stated that many students in this group remain unidentified because their gifts mask their weaknesses. Based on this they slip under the radar and thus go though education undiagnosed. According to Brody and Mills (1997), gifted students with subtle learning disabilities (e.g. students with exceptional verbal skills, but poor spelling and handwriting) are usually never identified as learning disabled. It is crucial to identify these difficulties early on, given that the gap between what is expected of these learners and their actual performance often widens, as they advance through school (Fetzer, 2000). The hidden gifted/learning-disabled group is even more challenging to identify, as their high intelligence works to compensate for their learning disability; however, their disability prevents their high intelligence from shining.

2. METHOD AND RATIONALE

The rationale of the intervention is fundamentally based on identifying the pupils' strengths and weaknesses in order to promote his strengths and work with his weaknesses. According to a survey performed by Robinson (1999), there are two factors that successful adults with learning disabilities feel have contributed to their success: a) knowledge of their own strengths and weaknesses and b) change in the perception of themselves and their learning characteristics from one of failure to a more positive, balanced view of having strengths as well as weaknesses. Hence, their own attitudes and feelings toward themselves and their abilities were the most important factors leading to their ultimate success. Little (2001) concluded that self-efficacy and independence of learning should be emphasised in promoting gifted/learning-disabled students. Moreover, Bisland (2005) outlined key strategies that improve memory, organisation and written expression. Regarding his written organisation, we decided to mainly work with the written expression strategy called DEFENDS, brought forward by Deschler, Ellis and Lenz (1996). The steps are to decide on goals and theme, estimate main ideas and details, figure out best order of main ideas and details, express the theme in the first sentence, note each main idea and supporting points, drive home the message in the last sentence, and search for errors and correct.

2.1. **The importance of phonological abilities.** One of the key skills we worked on was his phonological abilities, as he himself was concerned about those and the baseline assessment also showed that he had deficits in this area. Moreover, Martschinke et al. (2001) found the ability to analyse and synthesise phonemes seems to have the largest influence on later reading and spelling successes. O'Connor and Jenkins (1999) showed that simple phonological strategies such as segmenting phonemes and rapid letter naming qualified as primary discriminators of reading disabilities, more reliably than more complex interventions.

2.2. **Promoting interest in Science.** The Society for Science & the Public (SSP) publishes *Science News for Students* that consist of a wide variety of articles, accompanied by an indication of the appropriate reading age and power words that aid the STEM literacy. The reading scores are calculated according to the Flesch-Kincaid algorithm, that weighs the number of syllables and words in each sentence and accounts for the punctuation used. It represents the anticipated number of years of education required to readily understand the article as a whole. Hence, only articles with reading age 7 were chosen for the pupil that was part of the intervention. Hence, there was a strong focus on literacy, since this has been the main focus of this intervention.

2.3. **Intervention Timeline.** The intervention was planned to consist of seven weekly, half-an-hour long sessions with one pupil. Due to time contraints, the intervention had to be contrained to six sessions, as outlines below (see Figure 1)

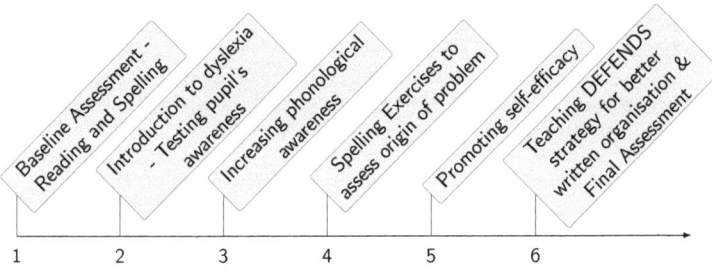

FIGURE 1. Intervention Timeline

2.3.1. *Baseline Assessment.* In order to test his reading and spelling ability and aiming to promote his interest in Science at the same time, the pupil was given a choice of three different science articles (*Science News for Students*) of reading age 7, that were followed by a list of power words. The three topics of choice were 'Gravitational Waves', 'Black Holes' and 'Cool Jobs: Exploring the Solar System'. The pupil was asked to read through his article of choice ('Gravitational Waves') out loud to control specifically for reading speed and pronunciation of words. He was then given 10 min to summarise the article in his own words. During this summary exercise, he was given access to a list of key words, as they were very challenging, e.g. 'interferometer'. After this exercise, he was asked to check his spelling. I then intervened and circled all the misspelt words according to the school's marking policy. He was then asked to improve his spelling with my assistance (see Figure 2).

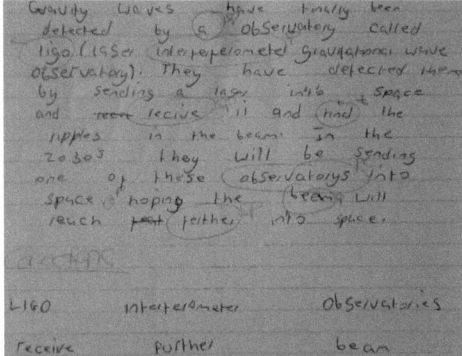

FIGURE 2. Pupil's summary on Science News article
about discovery of gravitational waves. Corrections were
suggested by me to promote further progress.

Evaluation. This session served to promote his interest in science and
to get a first overview of his strengths and weaknesses. I could identify
that he has no difficulty with reading. He mentioned to me that he
had particular issues with spelling words with vowels.

Next Step. As he expressed particular difficulties with spelling vowels,
I was able to do more research into different subtypes. It seems that the
dysphonetic dyslexia subtype seems to be the most close fit based on
this simple screening session, given that in this condition vowel sounds
are also particularly troublesome (www.dyslexia.learninginfo.org). This
is fundamentally based in difficulties with auditory analytic-sequential
synthesis.

2.3.2. *Assessing the pupil's awareness of implications of dyslexia.* As
there are not many dyslexics that are open about their difficulties,
a cartoon video that described the everyday impact of dyslexia in a
pupil's life was shown. The aim of using this objective medium was to
enable the pupil to understand that he - most likely - belongs to a large
group of individuals that struggle with similar problems, but that this
is independent of his intelligence. After this, the pupil was introduced
to Davis reading techniques, promoting his strength in reading. We
spent 10 more minutes to work with Davis reading techniques on the
'Black Holes' article. The Davis reading techniques help to improve
reading fluency and spelling accuracy. The techniques used here were
'Spell-Reading' and 'Sweep-Sweep-Spell': The pupil is asked to read
a passage out loud in the company of his support person. When he

encounters an unfamiliar word, he spells it out letter by letter. After
he says the name of the last letter, if he understands the word, he says
the word, and then moves on. If he does not understand the word,
his helper supplies it for him, the student repeats the word and then
continues.

Evaluation. This session served to make him aware of the everyday
experiences of a dyslexic pupil in an objective manner. He seemed
to identify with some of the mentioned struggles: however, he also
seemed to be slightly frustrated with the mentioned aspects of dyslexia.
Moreover, he knew about dyslexia, given that his sister had already
been diagnosed. I aimed to put a clear emphasis on his strengths,
pointing out to him that he was evidently good at reading. Therefore I
aimed to increase his self-esteem by continuing to work on his strengths
in literacy as well as addressing his spelling weaknesses in a constructive
way based on the Davis reading and spelling exercises.

Next Step. Based on my literature research (see Introduction), I aim
to improve his phonological awareness, as this has been outlined as the
crucial drive for improving the condition.

2.3.3. *Increasing phonological awareness.* In order to improve his phonological awareness, we worked though a list of trigger words (compiled
by Davis) and the English alphabet code, which relates simple phonemes to different, more complex graphemes. First of all, the pupil's
prior knowledge of phonemes was assessed more closely by strategic
questioning. He had not been aware of the English alphabet code.
Therefore the English alphabet code was introduced to him. Moreover,
he was made aware that English spelling is very challenging given that
English orthography is alphabetic but highly non-phonemic. Furthermore, the pupil was asked to spell a selection of Davis trigger words
(e.g. homophomes such as their/there/they're). An example list is
illustrated in Figure 3.

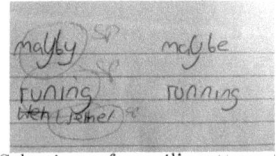

FIGURE 3. Selection of pupil's attempts at spelling
Davis trigger words independently with corrections based
on seeing the actual spelling.

The pupil was given a choice for the second task. Based on his great visuo-spatial skills, the pupil was asked whether a visual representation of trigger words with clay or conversation with teacher would be most beneficial. He decided it would be best for the teacher to dictate sentences and correcting them together, after the pupil had written them down in order to point out how this phonemes are spelt in different contexts (see Figure 4).

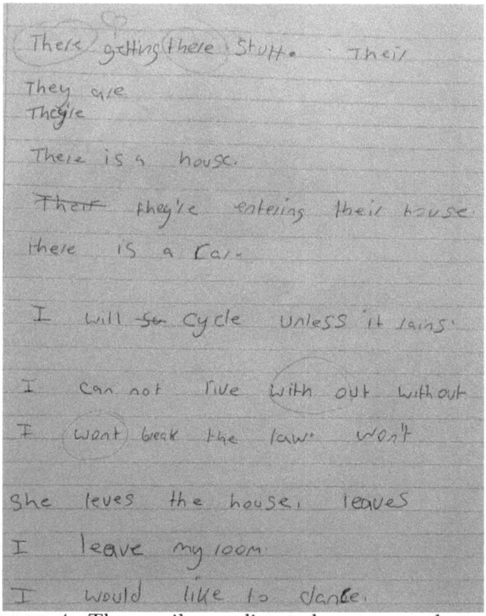

FIGURE 4. The pupil was dictated sentences that contain Davis trigger words, especially homophomes. Corrections were demanded by me to promote further progress.

Evaluation. This session revealed that he clearly struggled with many of the trigger words (see Figures 3 and 4). According to Davis, the mastery of these trigger words can prevent the disorientation that many dyslexics experience.

Next Step. He took the list home to practice with it, so that we could practice spelling in the consecutive session.

2.3.4. *Spelling exercises.* In the following session, we worked with different spelling exercises to assess the origin of the problem further. These spelling exercises can be described as follows:

- "Look Say Cover Write Check Say": The child looks at the word, says the word aloud, covers it, writes it from memory and checks to see if it is correct. Finally the child says the word again.
- Simultaneous Oral Spelling (SOS): The child reads the word, then writes it saying the names of the letters as s/he writes them, he/she then checks the word and if correct the process is repeated. continues.

The outcome of one of these sessions is illustrated in Figure 5

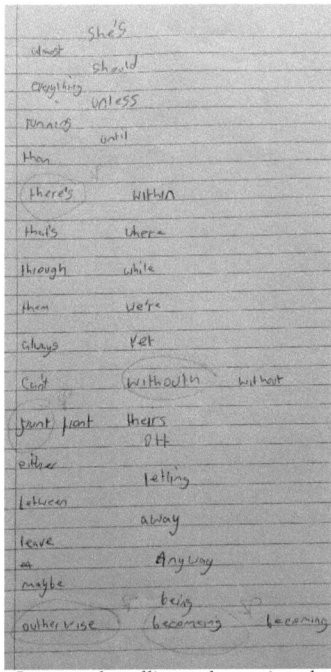

FIGURE 5. Improved spelling, when using the "Look Say Cover Write Check Say" method

Evaluation. He clearly performed much better at the Davis spelling exercises that provided extra scaffolding. Hence, we continued to work on his strengths by addressing his spelling weaknesses in a constructive way based on the Davis spelling exercises.

Next Step.   Based on my literature research (see Introduction), adult dyslexics declared that they profited most from a greater awareness of their strengths and weaknesses. Therefore the next session is dedicated to promoting the pupil's self-efficacy.

2.3.5. *Promoting his self-efficacy.* Following a short practice of the Davis reading and spelling exercises, the session was mainly dedicated to performing a SWOT analysis, i.e. declaring strengths, weaknesses, opportunities and threats (see Figure 6).

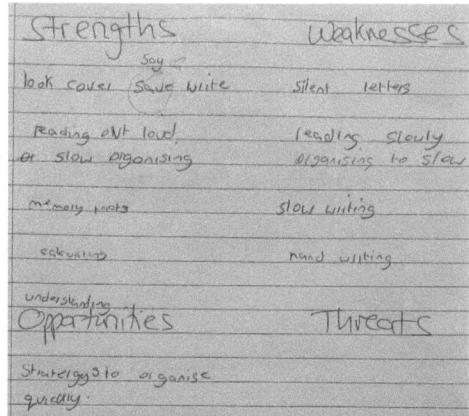

FIGURE 6. The pupil was asked to perform a SWOT analysis on his literacy skills. This has helped to increase his self-esteem, as he clearly excels in reading out loud as well as Davis spelling exercises. Moreover, his great understanding of Science was identified as one of his strengths. He identified himself that he is slower at reading and writing than his peers and that he needs to work on the legibility of his hand-writing.

Evaluation.   The pupil reacted very positively to praise as well as constructive feedback. He understood the rationale of this exercise and was very cooperative.

Next Step.   As written organisation was detected as one of his weaknesses, we spent the following session on the written expression strategy called DEFENDS, brought forward by Deschler, Ellis and Lenz (1996), followed by a final assessment.

2.3.6. *Teaching DEFENDS strategy for improved written expression & Final assessment.* In the final session, we practised the written expression strategy DEFENDS for a better overall organisation of his texts. The steps are to decide on goals and theme, estimate main ideas and details, figure out best order of main ideas and details, express the theme in the first sentence, note each main idea and supporting points, drive home the message in the last sentence, and search for errors and correct. Analogously to the baseline assessment, a choice of different science articles of reading age 7 was given to the pupil. This was also followed by a list of power words. The pupil was asked to read the article out loud to check reading speed and was then given 10 min to summarise the article according to the DEFENDS strategy. This was used to measure the impact of the intervention through comparing the baseline assessment with the final test performance (see Figure 7).

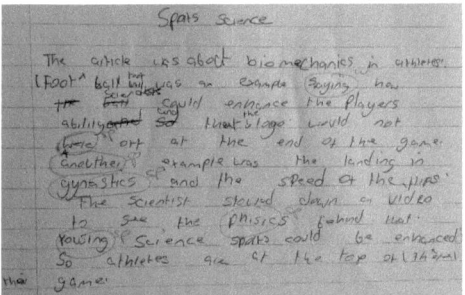

FIGURE 7. Pupil's summary on Science News article about Sports Science. As visible, pupil corrected some mistakes he spotted himself according to the DEFENDS method.

2.4. **Results.** In a Before-and-After studies comparison, the literacy error ratio improved from 15.78% to 9.46% (see Figure 8). When neglecting word-choice and punctuation errors, the pure spelling error ratio decreased from 12.29% to 6.7%. Moreover, the content was much better represented, according to the DEFENDS strategy. There is a clear introductory sentence, followed by mentioning the two examples that were given in the article, concluding with presenting the key message. When asked to feedback rate the value of this intervention, the pupil commented that it was helpful for him and that he appreciated the extra support.

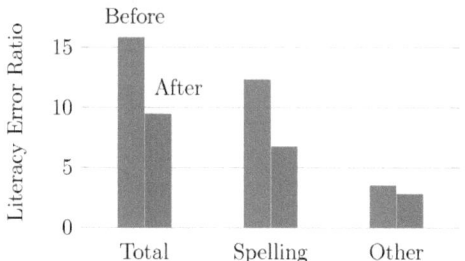

FIGURE 8. The literacy error ratio before and after the intervention respectively was calculated by dividing the number of erroneous words by the total number of words. Other mistakes include word-choice, tense and punctuation errors.

2.5. **Future Steps.** By having participated in the main intervention, the pupil has acquired a better understanding of his strengths and weaknesses in literacy, gained a greater self-efficacy and learned key skills that will help him to progress in the future. However, this short-term intervention will not be sufficient to ensure that the pupil remains on this current upwards-trajectory. Therefore he was given a workbook with different spelling exercises, that was highly recommended. I pointed out, which sections he should complete, e.g. a section on homophones, that were identified as one of his literacy weaknesses.

Image removed for publication due to copyright.

FIGURE 9. Excerpt on homophones from a spelling workbook called "Spellography" (Moats & Rosow, 2002) that student can use to self-assess his spelling in the future.

Moreover, using strategies to organise content in articles more quickly was identified as an opportunity in the SWOT analysis (see Figure 6). Evidently, the pupil has already profited from using the DEFENDS strategy in his final assessment (see improvements from Figure 2 to Figure 7).

3. Discussion

As the individual has two special educational needs it is twice exceptional, which has made the intervention more challenging. Regarding the methodology of this intervention, we need to consider whether there are any potential confounds in the study design.

3.1. **Before-After-comparison.** The effectiveness of the intervention was investigated using a 'Before and After' design, i.e. the same student was tested twice using the same procedure. The only potential confounds that might distort the results are the problems of temporal change, regression to the mean and insignificant sample size. Regarding the issue of temporal change, we need to ask ourselves whether there are any identifiable time trends (apart from the intervention) which are likely to distort the results. Regression to the mean describes that things, left to themselves, tend to return to normal, normalising extreme scores (high as well as low) on tests over time. These two effects are not as relevant in this study, given that the temporal duration was fairly short, only two months on the whole. Regression to the mean is most likely a negligible factor. Furthermore, the sample could have been too small, as it was a summary containing fewer than 100 words. However, due to the time constraints it was not possible to extend the respective tests.

3.2. **Challenging timings of sessions.** According to Hooper (2000), a dyslexic child is generally more tired than his peers by the end of a school day, because everything requires more thought, tasks take longer and nothing comes easily. Therefore more errors are likely to be made. Given that the pupils was only available during lunch break, it was very hard for him to focus during the sessions. If we had chosen a different time, he might have been able to make even more progress during the sessions. The first three sessions before the spring break took place at weekly intervals, whereas the last three sessions after spring break took place on three consecutive days, as these were the only three days I was present at the school.

3.3. **Potential diagnosis through administration of Boder test.** Due to the time and financial constraints, it was not possible to fully assess his condition. According to Boder and Jarrico's (1982) test, the different subtypes of dyslexia, i.e. dysphonetic, dyseidetic, and mixed criteria, can be investigated based upon specific reading and spelling patterns in different tasks.

3.3.1. *Methodology of the test.* The Boder Test of Reading-Spelling Patterns (BTRSP) consists of graded lists of 20 words that children are required to read out. They vary in phonological complexity and thus make it possible to assess the individual's main difficulties.

3.3.2. *Potential disadvantages.* Based on Hooper (1988), the reading section of the BRTSP is reliable, as the outcomes of pupils are linked with their scores on the Stanford Achievement test; however, they are not linked for the spelling section, i.e. pupils perform significantly worse in the BTRSP than in the renowned Stanford achievement test. According to different reviews, there are also flaws regarding the standardisations. Therefore it might not be the best choice to assess this specific individual's abilities.

3.4. **Building more strongly on his creative skills.** If more time had been available, it would have been useful to build on his very strong creative skills. His skills were clearly demonstrated, when he built a wooden boat as part of his homework to investigate buoyancy. Therefore, it would have been great to promote his self-esteem by building on his strengths.

4. Impact on Teaching Practice

Having done more independent research on dyslexia, I became more aware of the difficulties that dyslexic pupils face. Therefore, I have attempted and will continue to modify my teaching practice based on this newly gained knowledge, for example using more visual representations of learning content and providing more scaffolding when completing written tasks.

4.1. **Verbal rather than written explanation.** As dyslexic children are significantly more able to give information verbally rather than writing down thoughts and ideas, it is crucial for teachers to accept verbal descriptions as an alternative to written descriptions if appropriate, as the pupil must be able to demonstrate to the teacher that he knows the information and where he is in each subject for successful integration.

4.2. **Marking of work.** I have always aimed to give credit for effort as well as achievement due to my support of the growth mindset philosophy. Moreover, spelling mistakes pinpointed should be those appropriate to the child's level of spelling, rather than marking all spelling mistakes, which can be very disheartening for the child, when they have inevitably tried harder than their peers to produce the work. Therefore I focus on ensuring correct spelling of Science key words.

4.3. **Handwriting.** In future, I will continue to encourage dyslexic children to study their writing and to be self-critical, i.e. making them decide for themselves where faults lie and what improvements can be made, so that no resentment is built up. Moreover, I will continue to discuss the advantages of good handwriting and the goals to be achieved with the class. When giving them one-on-one support, I will analyse common faults in writing, by writing a few well chosen words on the board.

4.4. **In the classroom.** Of value to all children in the class is an outline of the success criteria in the lesson, ending with a resume of what has been learned. In this way information is more likely to go enter long term memory. For pupils with poor visual memory, additional support sheets are crucial.

5. CONCLUSIONS

Based on the baseline assessment, we found that the individual is 'twice exceptional' and most likely belongs to the subtle gifted/learning-disabled group based on the dysphonetic dyslexia subtype. The depicted intervention was based on identifying his strengths and weaknesses and successfully developed his literacy skills, especially his phonological awareness, as well as his interest and understanding of science simultaneously. The effectiveness of the intervention was assessed using a Before-and-After comparison of a written summary. The pupil made fewer spelling mistakes and was able to correct them independently. More precisely, the literacy error ratio, as calculated by dividing the number of erroneous words by the total number of words, improved from 15.78% to 9.46%. Moreover, the overall structure of his summary was better organised based on the DEFENDS method he was taught during the intervention. Therefore, this intervention can be seen as the first step in the right direction to support this individual's progress; however, it is crucial that a long-term intervention takes place.

REFERENCES

Benbow, C. P. and L. L. Minor (1990). Cognitive profiles of verbally and mathematically precocious students: Implications for identification of the gifted. *Gifted Child Quarterly 34* (1), 21–26.

Bisland, A. (2005). Using learning-strategies instruction with students who are gifted and learning disabled. *Teaching Gifted Students with Disabilities*, 161.

Boder, E. and S. Jarrico (1982). The bodertest of reading-spelling patterns: A diagnostic test for subtypes of reading disability. *Grune and Stratton, New York*.

Brody, L. E. and C. J. Mills (1997). Gifted children with learning disabilities: A review of the issues. *Journal of learning disabilities 30*(3), 282–296.

Capel, S. A. (2005). *Learning to teach in the secondary school: A companion to school experience.* Taylor & Francis.

Davis, R. (2010). *The gift of dyslexia: why some of the brightest people can't read and how they can learn.* Souvenir Press.

Deschler, D., E. Ellis, and B. Lenz (1996). Teaching adolescents with learning disabilities. *Denver, CO: Love.*

Fetzer, E. A. (2000). The gifted/learning-disabled child: A guide for teachers and parents. *Gifted Child Today 23*(4), 44–50.

Hodge, P. (2000). A dyslexic child in the classroom. *Retrieved April, 1, 2016 from.*

Hooper, S. R. (1988). Relationship between the clinical components of the boder test of reading-spelling patterns and the stanford achievement test: Validity of the boder. *Journal of School Psychology 26*(1), 91–96.

Kinsbourne, M. and E. K. Warrington (1963). Developmental factors in reading and writing backwardness. *British Journal of Psychology 54*(2), 145–156.

Martschinke, S. (2001). *Diagnose und Förderung im Schriftspracherwerb.* L. Auer.

Moats, L. and B. Rosow (2002). Spellography.

O'Connor, R. E. and J. R. Jenkins (1999). Prediction of reading disabilities in kindergarten and first grade. *Scientific Studies of Reading 3*(2), 159–197.

Renzulli, J. (1986). The three ring conception of giftedness: A development model or creative productivity. *Cambridge. Cambridge Pres.(51–92).*

Renzulli, J. S. (1978). What makes giftedness? reexamining a definition. *Phi Delta Kappan 60*(3), 180.

Toll, M. F. (1993). Gifted learning disabled: A kaleidoscope of needs. *Gifted Child Today (GCT) 16*(1), 34–35.

Whitmore, J. R. and C. J. Maker (1985). *Intellectual giftedness in disabled persons.* Aspen Publishers.

YOUR KNOWLEDGE HAS VALUE

- We will publish your bachelor's and master's thesis, essays and papers

- Your own eBook and book - sold worldwide in all relevant shops

- Earn money with each sale

Upload your text at www.GRIN.com and publish for free